The Things We See

Written by Chemise Taylor

Illustrated by Alexis B. Taylor

I0389126

Published by Autism Learners, LLC

First Printing, 2022.

ISBN: 978-1-951573-47-8

www.autismlearners.com

Apple

Bed

Bench

Bird

Paper

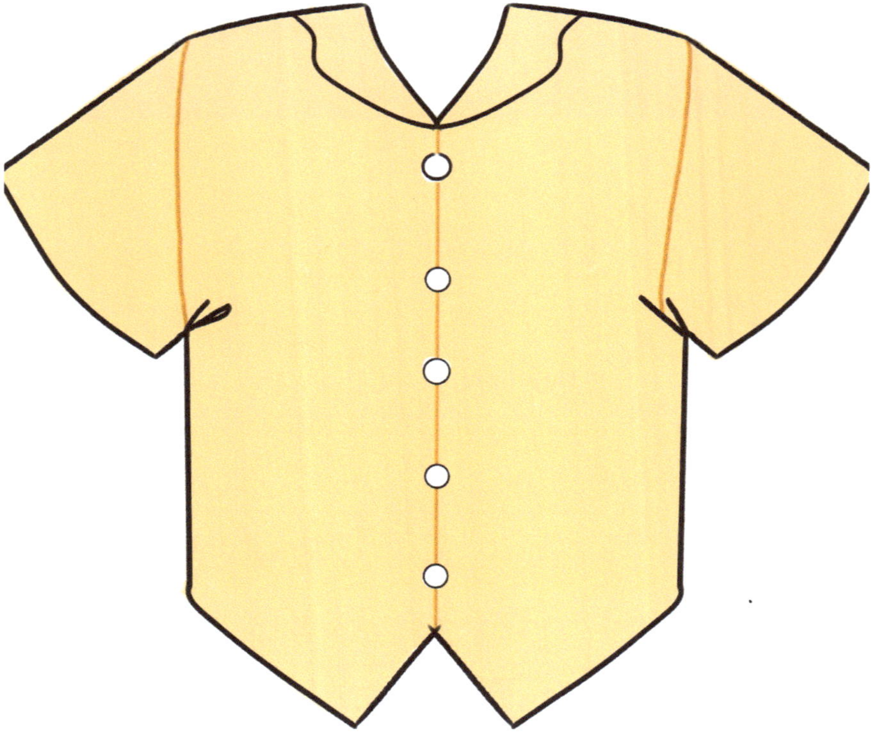

Shirt

Book Bag

Bread

Car

Carrot

Cat

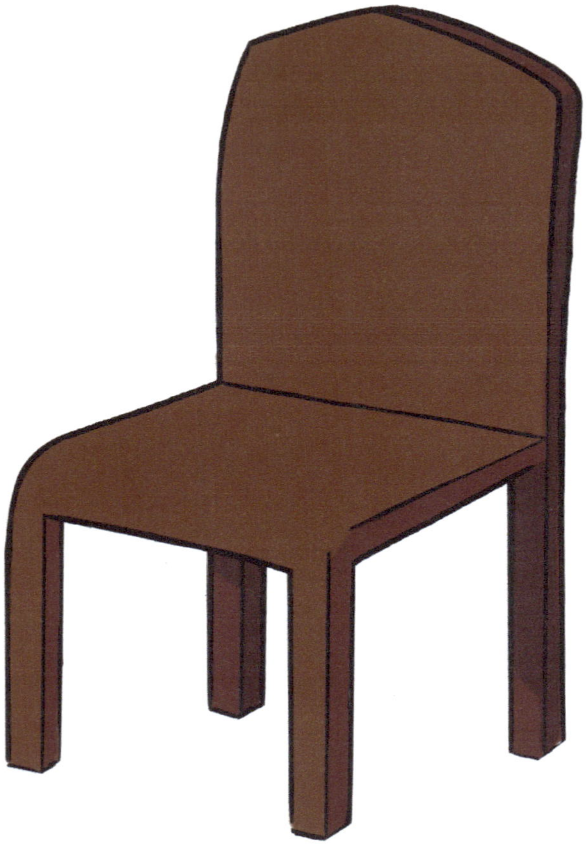

Chair

Coffee

Couch

Crayons

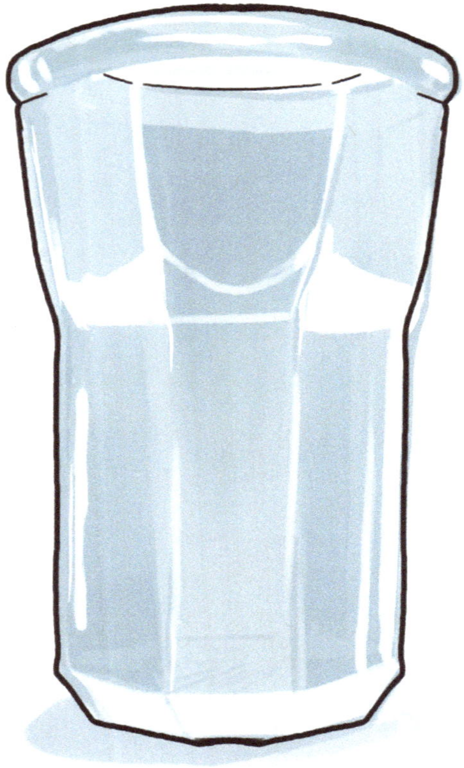

Cup

Dog

Dress

Fork

House

Keys

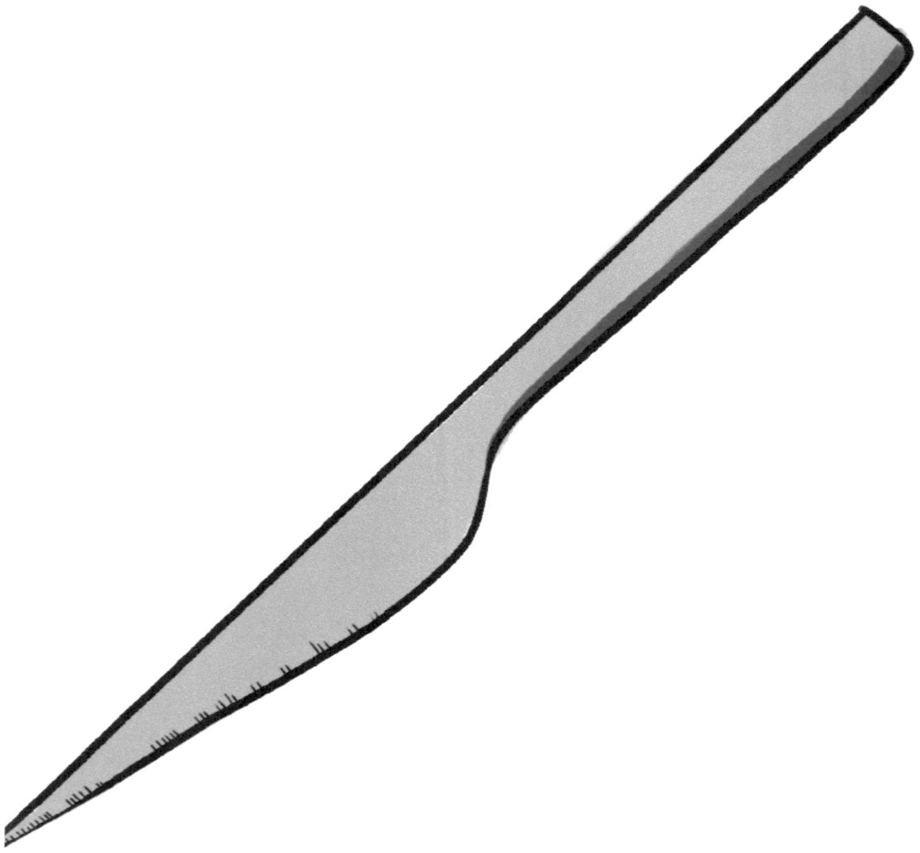

Knife

Lotion

Lunch Bag

Milk

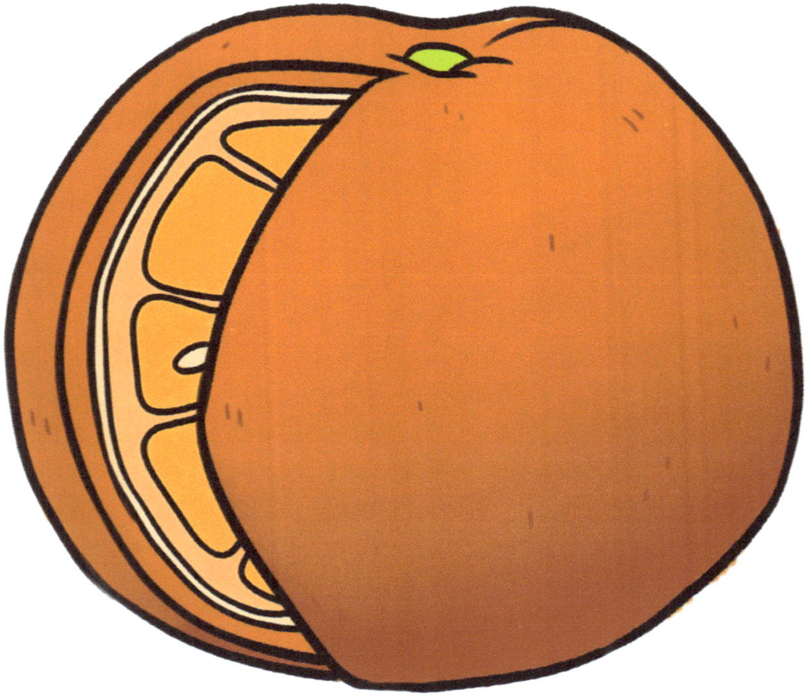

Orange

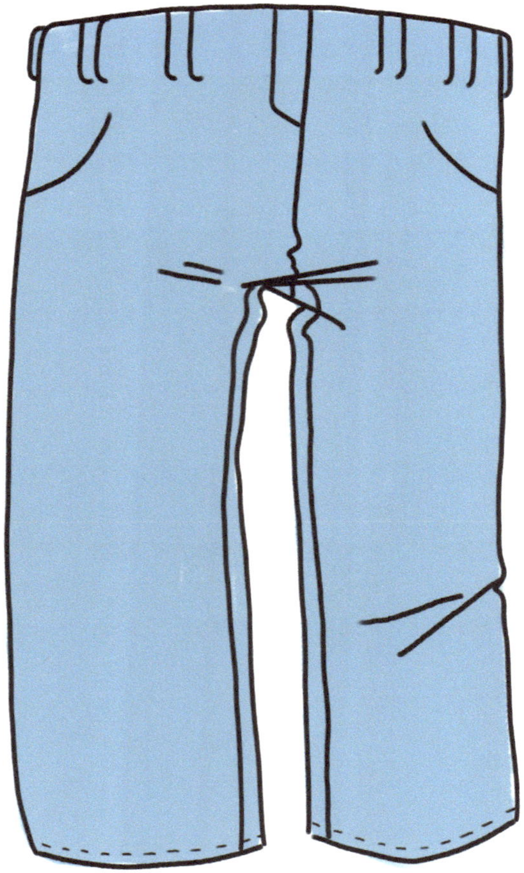

Pants

Pencils

Pillow

Soda

School Bus

Shoes

Socks

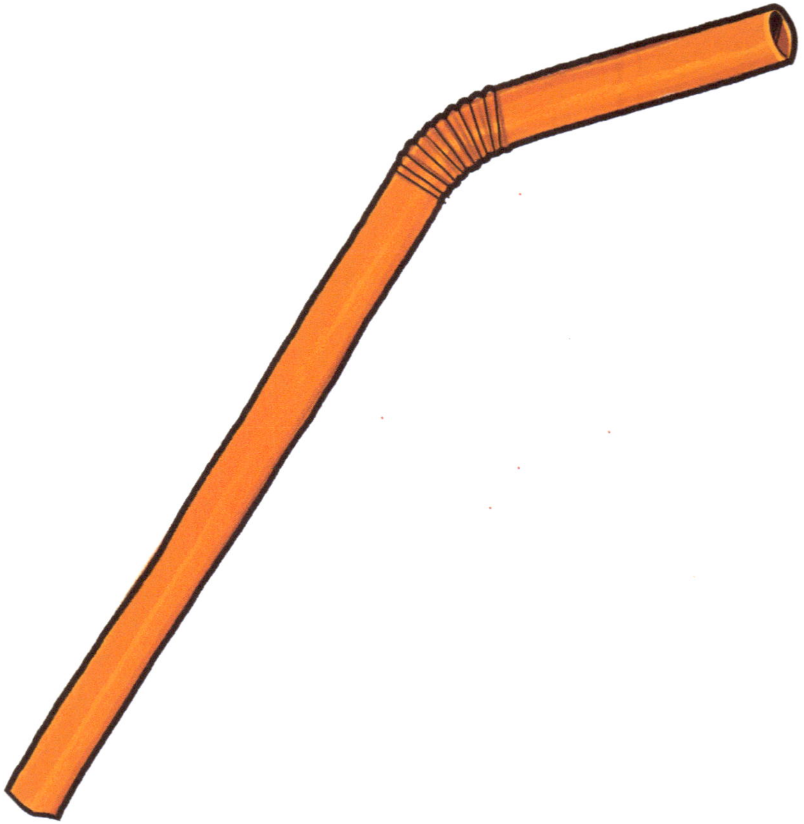

Straw

Table

Television

Locker

Tree

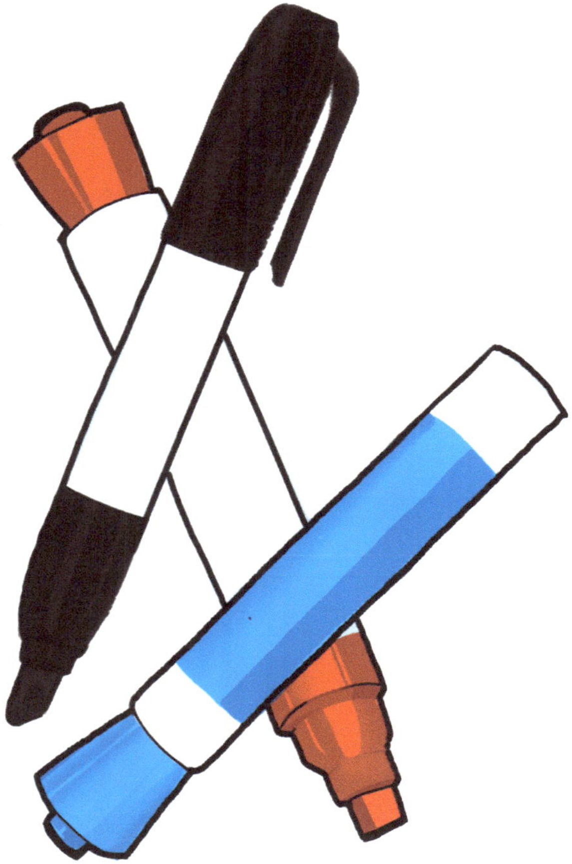

Markers

Desk

Whiteboard

Toothpaste

Water

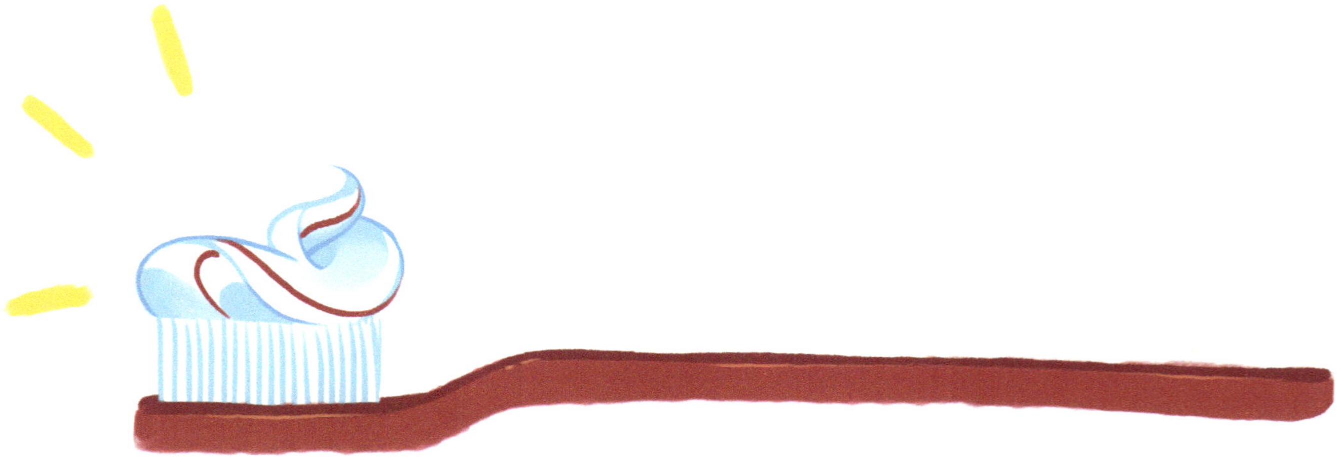

Toothbrush

www.ingramcontent.com/pod-product-compliance
Lightning Source LLC
Chambersburg PA
CBHW042110090526
44592CB00004B/67
9781951573478